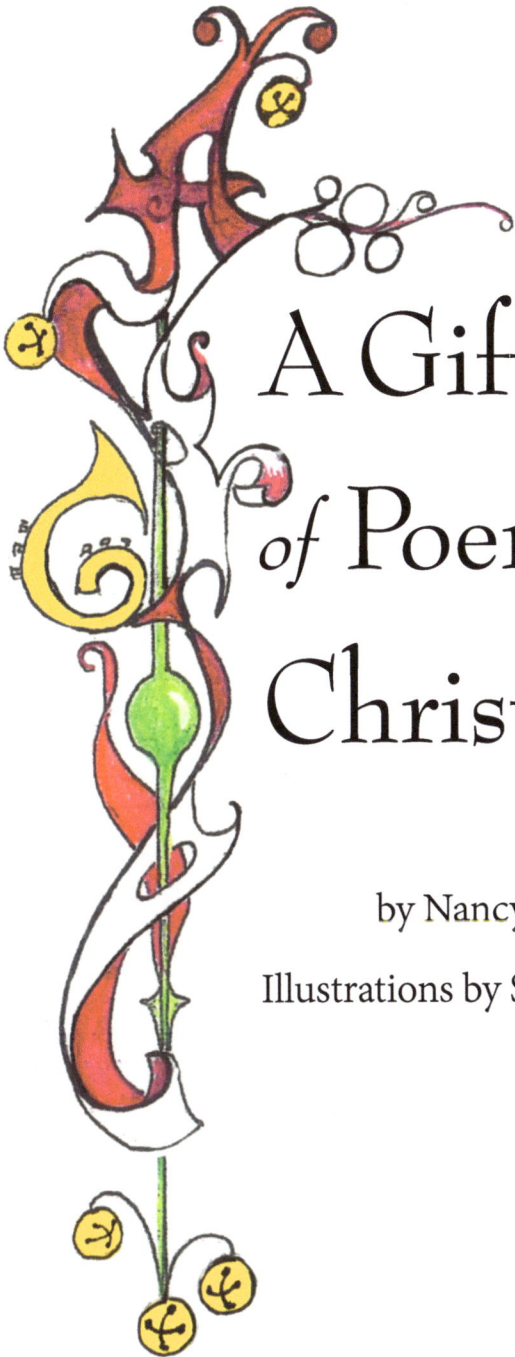

A Gift

of Poems *for*

Christmas

by Nancy K. Berry

Illustrations by Sally J. Steidel

Published by Berry Books
3202 Sunset Blvd.
Seaside, Oregon 97138

Printed in the United States of America
ISBN 978-0-615-96234-4

For

Our Families and Friends

∞

They are the ones
Who encourage and inspire us

PREFACE

In 1998, I wrote the first poem *The Christmas List* for my friends for Christmas. To my surprise, it was a much appreciated gift and long before the next Christmas, I was being asked if there would be another poem. Thus, a tradition was begun resulting in a collection of holiday poems. When friends began to ask for extra copies to use as gifts, it seemed logical to create a little book. However, I knew my writings would be enhanced in the hands of a gifted illustrator. Sally Steidel is that artist. She had loved the poems for some years and we both knew her style suited them perfectly. It is a pleasure to work with Sally and to watch my words come to life with her beautiful illustrations.

CONTENTS

The Christmas List

If I were the maker of lists this year,
the giver of gifts that bring good cheer,
these are the things I'd choose for thee and
they don't need wrapping for under the tree.

I'd give you the fragrance of cookies just baked,
the green of the lawn when the leaves are
all raked.
I'd send a jewel more precious than all—
that first yellow daffodil standing so tall.

The feel of the wind when you walk
on the beach,
the ripe juicy blackberry just out of reach
and laughter for sure, is a wonderful thing,
as a gift for a friend, it has a nice ring.

The flash of a Flicker quickly gone by,
the crimson and gold of a sun setting sky,
the sound of the waves as they rise and they fall
or the voice of a loved one on a long distance call.

I would pick for you from the gifts on my rack
the feel of the sun warm on your back,
the hand of a friend offered in love,
the twinkle of stars when you look up above.

So when you are choosing the gifts for your tree,
look at my list and I think you will see
why there's nothing at all that I'd rather do, than
share all these treasures with someone like you.

The Christmas Spirit

Christmas comes each year
no matter where you are.
It arrives in late December
hanging from a star.

You needn't have a tree
or a wreath upon your door.
It doesn't pick and choose
between the rich and poor.

It's a spirit warm and loving
that finds our hearts some way
and spreads across the land
like light at break of day.

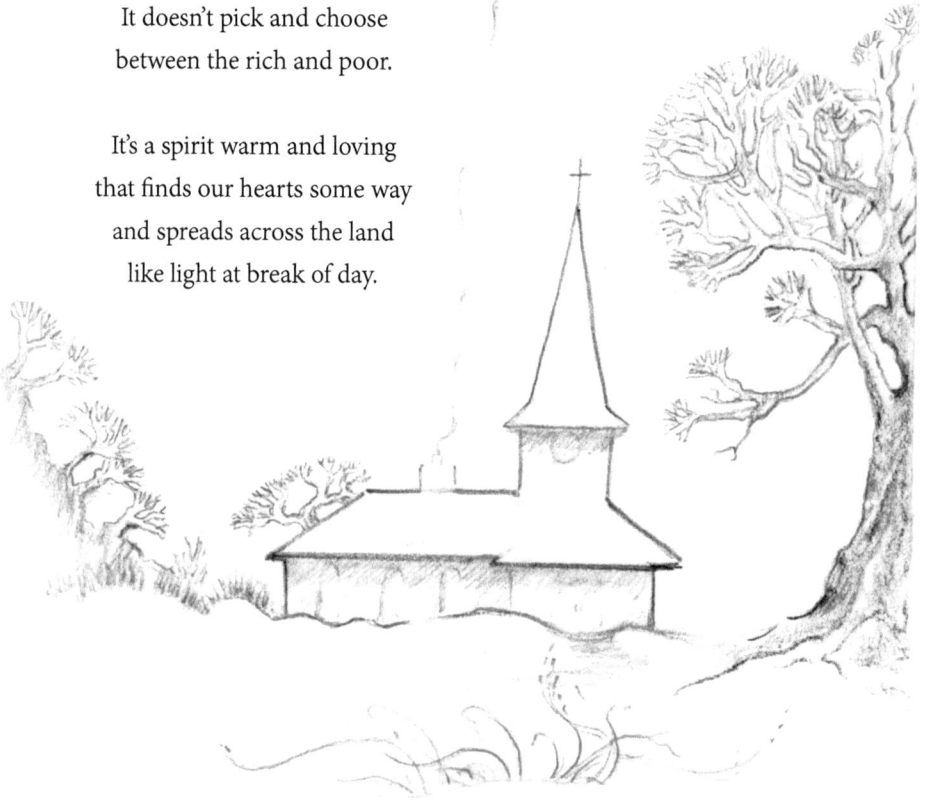

Even if we're lonely
or far away from kin,
reaching out in friendship
helps welcome Christmas in.

When Christmas comes this year,
I have a wish for you
may you find that loving spirit
the one that's Christmas true.

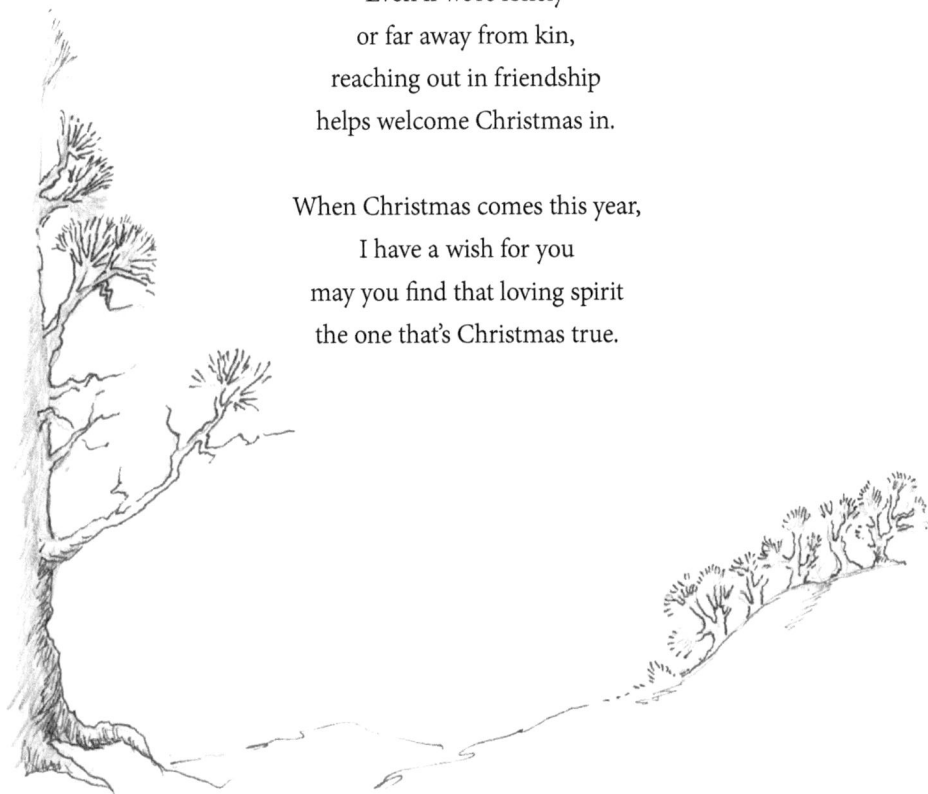

These are the Colors of Christmas
I Give to You

The green of the tree, the wreath and the holly
The red of the berries and the Santa so jolly

The brown of the cinnamon, nutmeg and cloves
The golden of goodness baked into loaves

The orange of oranges, the yellow of pear
The color of old bear that always sits there

The indigo sky on a clear winter's night
The gold of the star's pure shining light

The white of the snow for the color of love
They both change the darkness and
come
from
above.

A Baby So Small

The baby had promise, they said from the start
He was born of a miracle meant to change every heart.

But how could that be, some people did say, from
Such humble beginnings as a manger with hay.

Yet the prophets proclaimed a prince had been born,
A prince of the people, on that certain morn.

Herod just laughed, "It's only a star."
Then came three Wise Men traveling so far.

The shepherds claimed angels started to sing.
They came to the stable expecting a king.

But it was only a baby, a baby so small
It didn't seem likely he had promise at all.

Yet that little baby, a gift from above
Came with a promise, a promise of love.

And love's a strange thing as everyone knows
When you give some away, it grows and it grows.

That love's still around, there's plenty to share
Christmas is special 'cause it gets in the air.

We love one another and folks far and near
If only we'd do it all of the year.

Then we'd honor that baby, that baby so small
Who came with his love as a gift for us all.

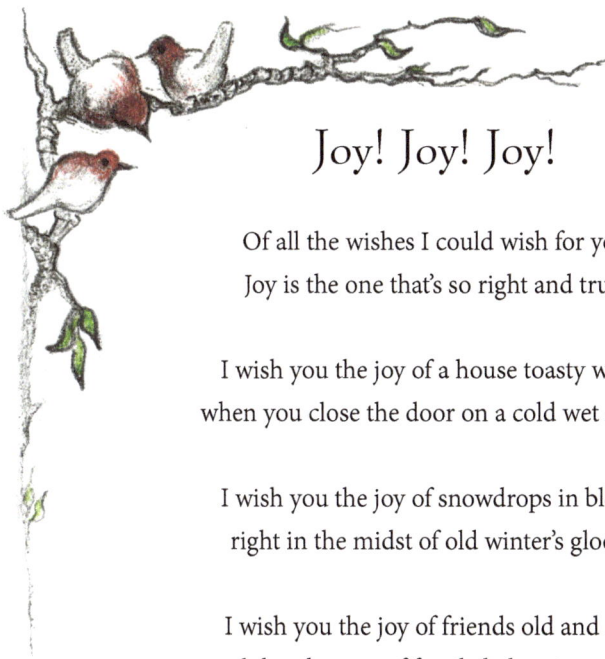

Joy! Joy! Joy!

Of all the wishes I could wish for you
Joy is the one that's so right and true.

I wish you the joy of a house toasty warm
when you close the door on a cold wet storm.

I wish you the joy of snowdrops in bloom
right in the midst of old winter's gloom.

I wish you the joy of friends old and new
and the pleasure of family belonging to you.

I wish you the joy of the hand of a friend
when you travel a road where you've not been.

I wish you the joy that a red finch brings
when he sits in your tree and happily sings.

I wish you the joy that makes you smile
and stays with you a long long while.

Joy is a Christmas word that we hear but
I wish you enough to last through the year.

Dear Santa

Dear Santa

When I was a child, our town was so small
no Santa resided at all in a mall.

So how did we tell him where we would be
and just what we wished to see under the tree?

We wrote him a letter to send in the mail
knowing that letters arrived without fail.

Our mother explained without much ado
one item's the limit for children like you.

There are so many children in a world so big
there's room for one each in that Santa sleigh rig.

We looked in Sears' book. We looked at the store.
We thought and we thought of what we wished for.

Those crookedy letters drawn with such care
were part of the magic we felt in the air.

That magic of Christmas, I wish for us all
when no Santa resided at all in a mall.

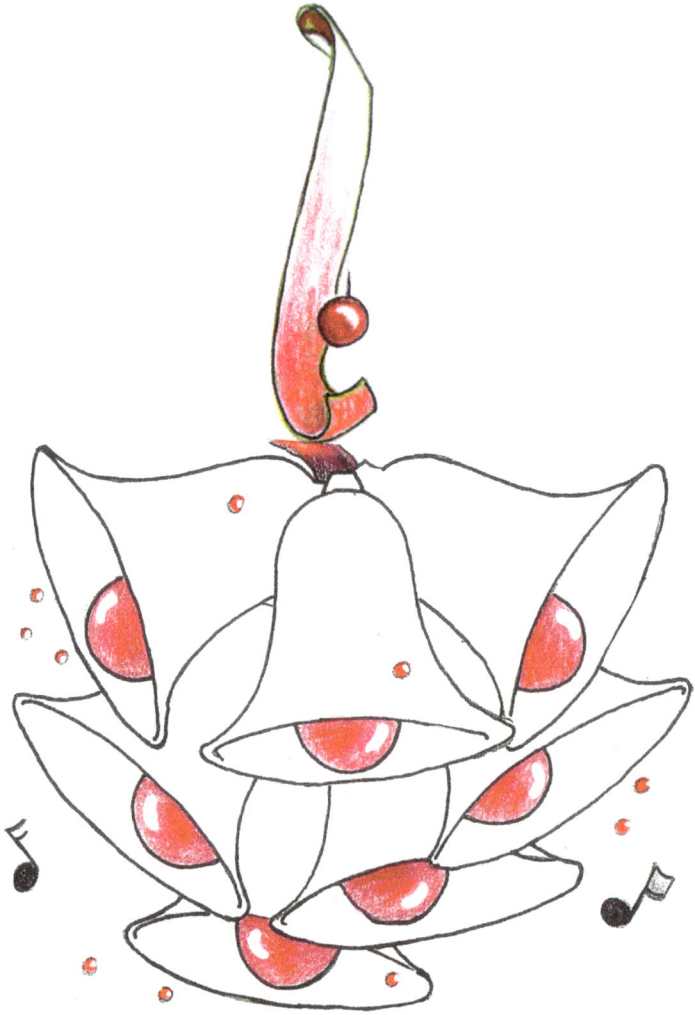

The Sounds of Christmas

Listen all around you, listen everywhere
For you know at Christmas, there's music in the air.
Music that we cherish, bells that ring good cheer
Favorite Christmas music—a pleasure every year.

That trite and tinny noise heard throughout the mall
Jingle bells still playing since early early fall.
Mother in the kitchen humming to herself
Father in the workshop playing Santa's elf.

Standing in the churches, their voices raised on high
People singing carols as Christmas time is nigh.
"Away In a Manger" perhaps the sweetest sound
Sung by little children, their voices newly found.

The Ho Ho Ho of Santa. Phone calls from afar
Wishing Merry Christmas, wondering how you are.
So listen all around you. I think that you will hear
The many sounds of Christmas, the ones we hold so dear.

Dove of Peace

The Dove of Peace has a broken wing
She feels so sad, she can't even sing
She worries about hunger, anger and strife
About all the children with a nobody life.

Oh what, little Dove, what can we do
This Christmas season to help heal you
Can one make a difference I ask, sweet bird
And deep in my heart, I thought I heard.

Begin with forgiveness of yourself and of others
Then think of the world as if we're all brothers
Kindness is next, it makes your heart grow
And that leads to charity as surely you know.

I have hope sighed the Dove, you'll heed what I say
And honor my wishes for this Christmas Day
Then perhaps I can heal and my wing can mend
So peace can be with us and the suffering end.

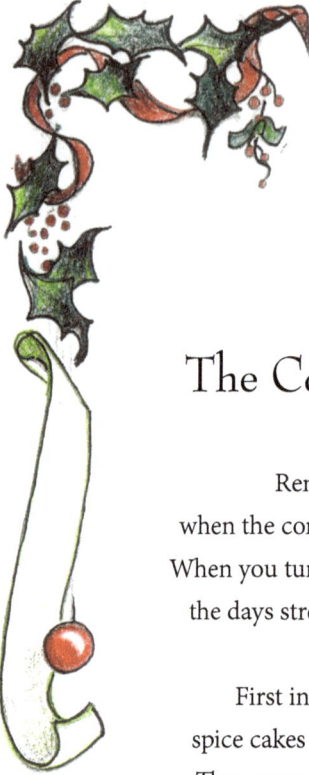

The Coming of Christmas

Remember a time so long ago
when the coming of Christmas was ever so slow.
When you turned the page, the page of December,
the days stretched endless. Do you remember?

First in the kitchen, the baking began
spice cakes and then cookies— pan after pan.
There were apples to peel, bowls to be licked,
popcorn was popped and favorites picked.

Whispers and secrets, gifts to be made
with scissors and paste. Maybe, allowances saved.

The tree was brought home and put in its stand.
No matter the size, it always looked grand.
The lights and the tinsel and finally the star
meant carols at church, cards from afar.

That excitement and joy would continue to grow
when the coming of Christmas was ever so slow.
If you remember, remember those times
you'll know what I wish for you with these little rhymes.

I wish you the wonder of a child aglow
at a Christmas long gone when its coming was slow.

The Light of Christmas

December is the darkest month
there seems more night than day
until the lights of Christmas
start shining bright and gay.

First the shops and city streets
spruce up with red and green.
Then the churches, every one
unpack the manger scene.

Soon the folks in neighborhoods
are stringing lights with cheer
and houses start to twinkle
when evening time is near.

Another light of Christmas
in heaven we do behold,
the precious Christmas star
more valuable than gold.

It brings us hope and comfort
no matter where we are
and lifts us from the darkness
that cherished star so far.

I wish for you a Christmas
filled with love and light
enough to last you thru the year
and keep you from the night.

The Christmas Garden

For a Christmas garden, what shall we grow?

For a Christmas garden, what shall we sow?

Let's start with charity for those in need
then along beside it plant a good deed.
I like compassion along the fence
and let it grow tall as well as dense.
In that dark corner to banish the gloom
we can put hope with its beautiful bloom.
Strength's a good tree standing so tall
spreading its branches and sheltering all.
Put lots of love down on the ground,
plant it in front so it can creep around.
Joy always bears flowers, bright and gay.
If we plant enough, we'll have a bouquet.
When the garden looks good, last but not least
scatter over all the seeds of peace.
If you plant these things and hold them dear,
your Christmas garden will last through the year.

A Christmas Stocking

I made for you this stocking
And filled it up with cheer
Plus other happy things
To last you through the year.

First I put in friendship
Because I like it much
To that I added humor
Giggling and such.

I would like to give you patience
But I'm always running out
So a little dab of tolerance
Will substitute no doubt.

Then I added beauty
From gardens or the beach
It wasn't too expensive and
It's always within reach.

With good health, love and peace
It was almost to the top
There were only two more things
And then I had to stop.

In all the nooks and crannies
I put New Year wishes true
Then piled on Merry Christmas
From my heart just for you.

Ready for Christmas

Are you ready for Christmas?
Is the refrain that we hear.
Are you ready for Christmas?
It's ever so near.

Are your cards in the mail?
Have you been to the mall?
We hustle and hurry
Doing it all.

Have you lights on the tree?
And a wreath for the door?
Can you help with this party?
Can't you do more?

As the days of December
Keep marching along
We sing "Hurry and Scurry"
For our Christmas song.

Then, at the very last minute
When the stockings are hung,
At the very last minute
When everything's done.

We are finally reminded
What we knew from the start
That the place to be ready
Was here in our heart.

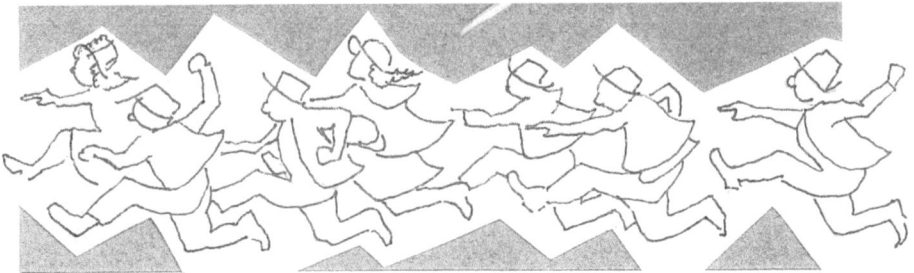

Gifts to Give

Have you that list, that list that tends
to name some gifts for special friends?
Before you go further, here are some thoughts.
They're only ideas, not really "oughts."

Give CHEER
A little cheer goes a long long way
to help us all throughout the day.

Give FORGIVENESS
Just in case you've been really mad
at someone close who's done something bad.

Give EMPATHY
Put yourself in another's shoes.
There's so much to gain and nothing to lose.

Give FRIENDSHIP
Cherish a friend, a new one or old, and
both lives will be filled with riches untold.

Give PEACE
Try to choose peace wherever you go.
A good Christmas gift for all that you know.

Give LOVE
Give freely of love and spread it around.
Nothing more precious will ever be found.

There you have it, my ideas galore
to simplify Christmas and make it mean more.
If in your heart, you tuck these away
Christmas will be there most every day.

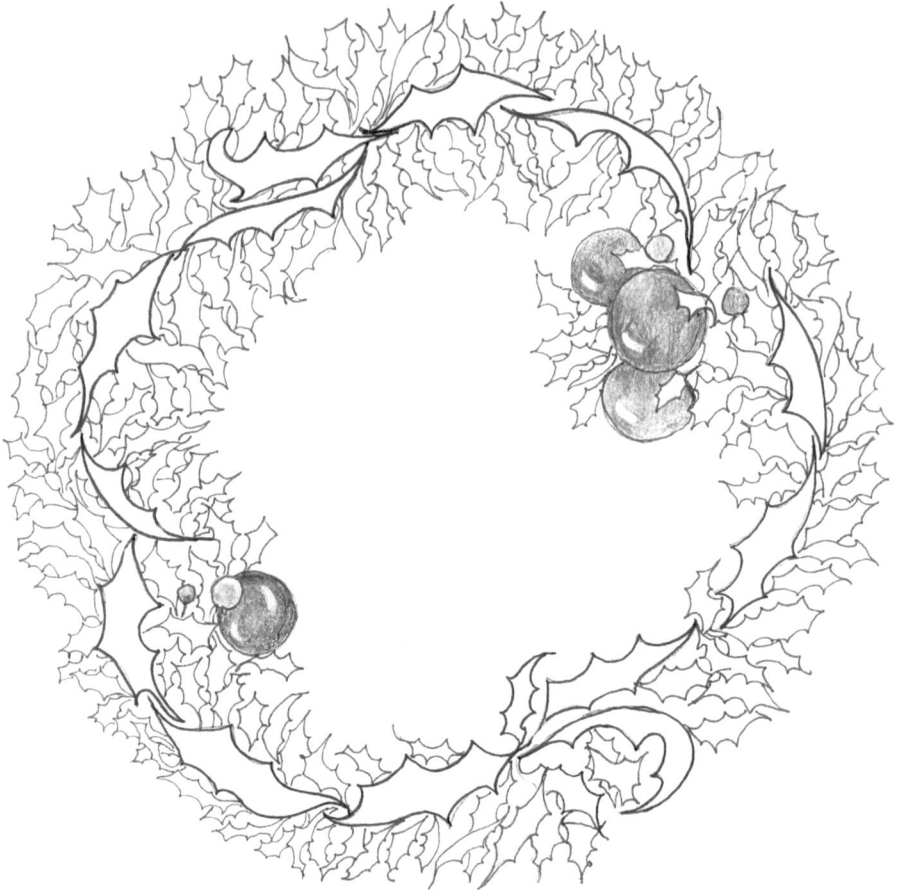

A Christmas Wreath

A Christmas wreath is a wonderful thing.
It hangs by the door and invites folks to ring.

It might be of pine with needles so fine
that in the porch light they practically shine.

Holly is jolly with its berries of red
or maybe fir is the one you opt for instead.

Or possibly spruce with a hue that is blue.
You could twist a grapevine, it's just up to you.

Stars and bells and Christmas bows
these are the things that everyone knows

Make your wreath special, a wonderful thing
to hang by your door and invite folks to ring.

Christmas Memories

Snowmen, Santas, Christmas trees
Stars and bells, all of these
Bring to mind the season nears
And we remember other years.

Always quick to come to mind
That Christmas pageant, we were nine
Those mice that jumped out from the hay
Just as we knelt down to pray.

The candy canes we made for fun
Knowing well when we were done
There'd be bits of taffy everywhere
On the floor and in our hair.

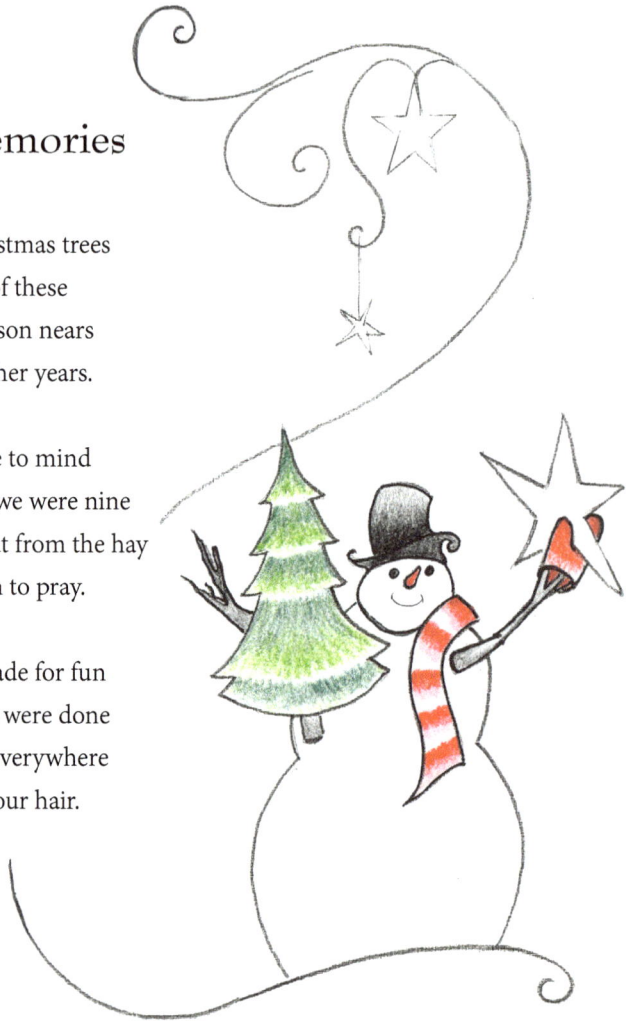

Home for Christmas that first time
When we moved out on our own dime
Remember the warmth of being back
Carrying your suitcase or your pack.

There was the year of the big snow
Driving home, grandbabe in tow
All the family paced the floor
'Til we pulled in at half past four.

We think of gifts our children made
With paste and paper in first grade
How they watched with eyes aglow
As we untied that loopy bow.

Christmas memories from the heart
Christmas memories, the best part
We take them out, turn them round
Each one seems a treasure found.

That is what I wish for you
Cherished memories, old and new
Having time this busy year
To remember all that's dear.

www.ingramcontent.com/pod-product-compliance
Lightning Source LLC
LaVergne TN
LVHW010029070426
835513LV00001B/29